Lunar Honey

Holly R. Toomer

Cleone Regine Publishing
New York

Lunar Honey

Copyright © 2021 by Holly R. Toomer
Cleone Regine Publishing

All Rights Reserved.

Published in the United States.

ISBN-13: 978-1-7372129-1-1

No part of this publication may be reproduced, stored in a retrieval system or transmitted in any form or by any means electronic, mechanical, photocopying, recording or otherwise, without the prior written permission of the author and publisher.

www.hollytbooks.tumblr.com
Bookings: cleonereginemgmt@outlook.com

Printed in the United States of America.

First Edition

Thankful for my heavenly Father, allowing me to breathe art.

This book is dedicated to my late mother Eloise Toomer and loving father Holland Toomer. Thank you for being a blueprint of love in earthly form.

To my best friends and family of creatives: thank you for supporting me, inspiring me and keeping me on my toes.

To my readers: don't let anyone make you believe that you are anything less than amazing. See my notes in the back in case you ever forget.

~ Holly

CONTENTS

LOVE-ISH

HIM..7
Inquisitive Mind....................................11
Ambrosial...13
Ego Fillin'..15
Kept...17
Central Air...20
Truth Serum..21
False Idols... 23
Confession #3..................................... 24
April Rain... 25
Fruit of Love....................................... 26
Reset...27
Soul D'Or..28
SapioLove...29
I Hope It's Love...................................31
When You Kiss Me..............................32
Female Alpha......................................34
The Keys...36

CONSCIOUS

Honey Commandment #1……………………..39
The Black Condition……………………………..40
Talking Heads……………………………………42
Confidant…………………………………………43
Four Shadows……………………………………44
Who Do You Do It For?..45
Afro Rebel………………………………………..47
Umoja……………………………………………50
Where You Belong………………………………51

ECLIPSE

The Solution…………………………………………53
Pep Talk……………………………………………..54
Don't Let Them…………………………………..56
Insanity……………………………………………57
Soul Food…………………………………………58
Headspace…………………………………………59
The Trap…………………………………………..60
Poetry Babe………………………………………62

DEAR READER AFFIRMING THOUGHTS

ABOUT THE AUTHOR

Holly R. Toomer

LOVE-ISH

Lunar Honey

HIM

Psychologist:

So, tell me.
Tell me more about—him.

Poet:

He understood,
That sometimes when I said I was good,
I was practicing speaking it into existence.
And no, Doc—
It was not resistance.
It's a concept that psychology has not quite depicted.
He kept me lifted,
In a love story that you'd think was scripted.
But it seems like my way back to him,
Has been encrypted,
And I'm password restricted.
I pass these words as witness to the verb,
I've been inflicted
With.

Psychologist: -- *And how does that make you feel?*

Lunar Honey

Holly R. Toomer

Lunar Honey

Inquisitive Mind

An inquisitive mind asking, why?
I don't want you to be perfect
I want you to try.
You know that it's worth it.
Butterflies undenied,
This addiction to high has no effect of sides.
Free falling out of the sky,
But we always jump back up and fly,
And jump back up always, one more time.
Because our story has no climax
No credits
The bond we have is unbreakable and embedded.
Fears of inadequacy you've dreaded,
Become irrelevant,
And although your concerns are benevolent
The masterpiece that you speak of
Is still—
Under development.
That all white you awed,
Is beautifully flawed,
And you being underqualified,
Is completely fraud.

But I always think, can I?

Be nothing more than an ally?
The bond is there, I can't lie.
But even when the tears dry,
An inquisitive mind is still asking, why?

Lunar Honey

Ambrosial

My Ambrosial Honey
Couldn't help but get stuck.
Grew up on opposite sides of the track too,
Who would've thunk?
But those seem to be the facts that make us
Perfect for
Each
Other,
And I
Don't want
Another.
I love you like
My brother
Treat you like my friend, my thoughts of you
Transcend
To the Third Heaven.
I'm back
And for you
I'll bend
Our scuffles
I'll amend
And although
The depths of my sensations I can't quite comprehend
I'll pretend

That I'm cool...

Ego Fillin'

Unapologetically virtuous
I spoke life into you.
Had your trust and attention,
I gave you views.
Had your love fueled ascension,
I was,
Your muse.

With me
You didn't have to try.
The joy
Just
Was.
Happy in each other's presence
I love you,
Just
'Cause.

Egos don't fill voids,
But they do stretch,
And this is where my boldness
Comes into effect.
Why are you looking for puzzle pieces
When I've already

Completed you?
We've both said some things
We didn't mean.
I'll be the first to say
I'm sorry, too.

Lunar Honey

Kept

You are beautiful
The way your eyes lay on top of your cheeks when you smile,
The way your forehead wrinkles when I say something wild,
And I could kiss
Each one
of your battle scars if you let me.
Aid your happy
If you let me
If you—
Let me.

I'm just waiting on you to
Bet me
Time keeps on slippin' but I wish you would have kept me.
Can I carry your load in prayer and make them burdens lighter?
I just want to see the light in your eyes bright-up
'Cause I never
Ever
Want you to lose sight of—
The God in you

Being true
And I love how you love
From the rebel in you.
But anyway
I'm just all the way in the clouds
And these stars need to chill
Because weeks pass by
And you're on my mind still
FRESH
Like your lips are still holding mine.
Blessed.
Why you gotta be so fine?
Why you gotta be so, FINE?
Couldn't tell what you've been through
You age like wine
And I'd want you even if you gained 20 pounds.
'Cause it's not really looking at you that drives me crazy
But
When
You
Speak
I thank the one who made you.
I thank the fear He gave you.
'Cause you have enough substance
To feed my soul

For a couple of forevers.

Lunar Honey

Central Air

I love you,
Even in the not so warm spaces,
When it feels like,
I'm laying next to the AC unit,
But because my love is not conditional,
I stay,
Double-up the blankets,
And tuck us both in.

Lunar Honey

Truth Serum

I cared too much.
A truth that could be acknowledged now
'Cause I've finally laid the problems down
That were blocking my view
Of you.
A truth
It's true
I knew.

I would travel miles for you
Quite literally
And some might say silly of me
Because frankly
You didn't ask me to—
It's true
Crimson hearts turn blue.
Sometimes you simply fall in love
And forget that it takes two.

It's true
And it's cool
'Cause of what that thing
They say
The truth could do for you

And it did.

Lunar Honey

False Idols

Say won't you just show me the real you? I'm a poet not a judge, but I will give you a sentence or two. How does one learn how to love when authenticities become taboo? And there goes you. And there goes you.
Don't know what's true, false idols.

Having a pure heart comes with affliction.
False Idols
Most of what they say to you is fiction.
My prediction?
You'll become akin to what you hate if you don't fix them.
Counterfeit love places felicity on restriction.
Benediction
Guard your heart,
Or it's peace you'll be missing
For out of it flows the issues of life
Desist constrictions.
False Idols
Bc mindful,
Of the interest that they keep.

Confession #3

I couldn't let myself go to you.
Balance is a fluid state,
I couldn't let myself flow to you.

Lunar Honey

April Rain

In this season,
You are the reason,
I wear black so much.
Left in pieces—
Rest in peace is
What I said to your touch
Because it was all in vain.
And each time I hear your name,
I feel
All
In
Pain
These pictures I have left of you
Don't look back at me the same.
This is the true rain that April brings.
You see,
Love moves adversely if not used as directed.
Fulfilling my residency
Until
It's perfected.

Fruit of Love

I don't want to control your thoughts of me,
That's called
Manipulation.
Authentic is what this ought to be,
It's a good thing that I'm
Patient
And Kind.
I'm trying
To be the purest form of Love.
The kind that is forgiving
Although I can't give up a son,
I did give up the habits of a girl who's on the run
From The One.
The One.
The One soul I could connect with.
I've rejected
And been left with
Reflected pieces of what broke in me.
I thank the Creator for the light and key
To breaking what's been holding me.
I'm
Finally
Free.

Lunar Honey

Reset

I am your reset button.
Forget everything that you thought you knew about love, Love.
Because in the past, for pain
You were a glutton.
You've never made love,
You were just nuttin'
And I'd be frontin'
If
I told you
That I'm not scared
With you.
But over time I've realized that
Fear never really leaves
But goes
With you.
Some details make it complicated
And it could all be so simple
But before we do
Can we just promise
To hit reset
Then
Play.

Soul D'Or

She is a skillful
Lover and warrior.
So, please do not invade
Unless your intentions
Are pure.
I beg of you
Not for her sake
But yours.
For if she should love and leave you
There won't be a woman
You wouldn't look through her for.

SapioLove

I love to be
And your misses.
You are the
Greatest planter of third eye kisses
Known to have the other 4 to 5 of my senses
Wishin'
They could all experience you
At the same time.

You are constantly on my brain,
So much so,
That my subconscious and conscious mind
Instantaneously agree,
On the subject of you.

Lunar Honey

I Hope It's Love

What are these
Things
Commingling with the blood inside my veins
Fluttering through my hands and
lower tummy
My words
They run from me
And I feel as If I've been found out every time
someone says your name
Or even just a name that sounds the same
Like do they know what I'm thinking?
And would that even be so bad?
I clearly need some assistance
After rushed experiences I've had
My predisposition?
To connect with nomads
But I'm so glad
None of the flags
Are red

When You Kiss Me

When you kiss me
I believe you.
When you kiss me
It lets me know that every decision I've made in my life,
Till this moment,
Must have been correct—
Because it led me,
Here
With you
And this I know,
Is right.
When you kiss me,
I understand my role through this plight,
And in that of our success.
When you kiss me,
I believe you when you tell me I'm the best
And I will always aim for better,
Even when it's worse.
When you kiss me,
We break every generational curse.
I heard the mountains ask how far we want them to move.
When you kiss me,

Lunar Honey

We make them rough patches smooth,
When you
Kiss me.

Female Alpha

She doesn't have—the time.
Many men out here know that she's fine,
And they're not sprung from her looks,
They've read the good book
And they know that a woman's truest treasure
Lies deep.
Beauty on the surface
Is weak.
That's not where she peaks,
Words of life she speaks,
Because there's a divine being within she,
And when you're in tune with the Most High,
"Just enough" won't get by.
She doesn't have—the time.
Call her
Female Alpha
Virtuous in demeanor
Know her when you see her
The souls she's awoken
With wisdom spoken
Kindness
Is her token
Her ambition
Can't be broken

Lunar Honey

And for the weak in spirit
She's outspoken.
So unless you're ready to take up your crown
And get in line?
She doesn't have—the time.

The Keys

I believe in interventions of the Divine
And I believe
That God put the keys to the universe between your bottom lip
And the top of mine

Lunar Honey

Holly R. Toomer

CONSCIOUS

Lunar Honey

Honey Commandment #1

Thou shalt know thyself.

The Black Condition

To live this life on the other side
The side that's veiled
Means,
Taking on multiple roles
Curating tales
From the sober
To the triumphant
Then wonder
How did we take three steps back?
To still disproving the seemingly impossible
To figuring out
How to bring our girls back.

It means,
It doesn't matter the credit hour
You make sure that
You learn enough
To take back power.
You learn enough
To fuel your dreams
Enough
Not to get trapped in these systematic themes.
You become the reporter of the news that's sober,
The alternative fact checking relative,

Lunar Honey

The counselor for emotional disorders.

You become the love that's bolder.

They set us up to lose integrity,
You make sure that you hold her.

Talking Heads

It's a wonder that we understand each other half of the time.
So many different conversations going on in each other's mind,
And to be honest
I get tired when you don't seem to be listening to mine.

Lunar Honey

Confidant

Come
Be
In the
Sky with me
Won't you get high with me?
Nah I don't smoke
But I do blow trees
Winds of knowledge
An embracing breeze
Strong enough to blow covers
Whatcha hidin'?
I saw you look for someone to confide in
Empty seat on that carpet you're ridin'
Tell me where your mind
Really
Is.

Four Shadows

You ever heard that saying?
If you hear something so much, you start to believe it?
God bless the children raised with
Harsh tones and grievance
Destined to live the words spoken over them —
Until the day, they are met with the counter argument.

Lunar Honey

Who Do You Do It For?

I move from my deep,
Cultivated by the power of the sun
And part of my destiny is to belt out stories unsung.

I do it for Langston,
Whose work knew no time,
'Cause in 2021 we're still ,
Caught between his lines,
That are modern day signs,
Of the black condition.

I do it for love—
I do it for the hope we can put this in,
Implementing Modern Day Abolition,
Because even today,
We are still targeted ,
With surgical precision.

And most importantly
I do it for the ones
Who don't know that they're slaves
Oblivious to those chains
That the world campaigns.

Holly R. Toomer

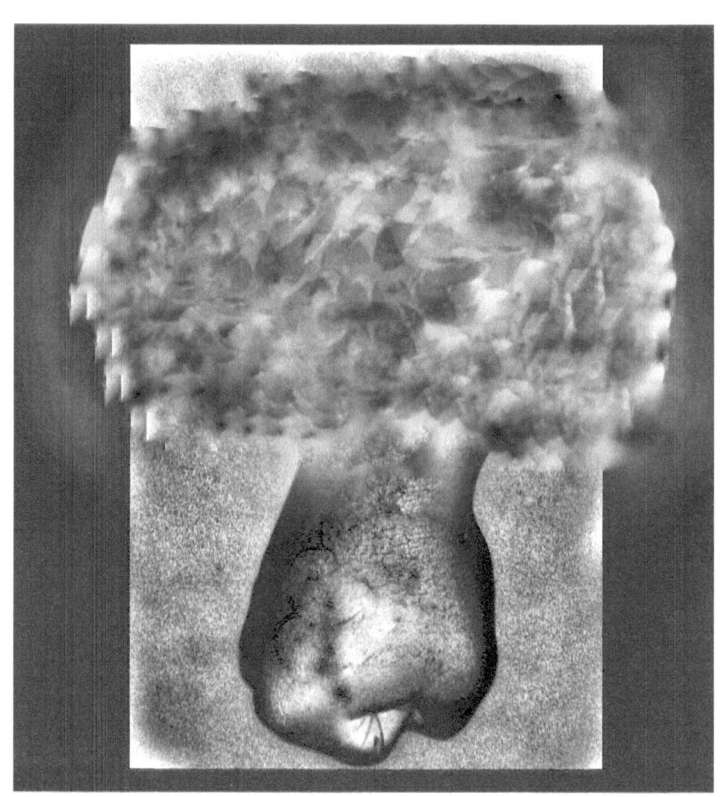

Lunar Honey

Afro Rebel

I move with purpose,
But I still take my time.
My spine
Is the true arch that's golden.
History unfolds in
This soft wool shrinkage,
Evidence of dynasty linkage.
My hips rest
Comfy on my thighs
Sitting for the ride
As I take each stride
Unapologetic and untried
And though my people they divide
Our love is amplified.
Divinity verified.
Let me make this clarified—
God's law is first and foremost.
I live not by the rules of men.
Because I knew I was never of this realm
Some call it rebell-ion
But tell me,
When it's man versus God
Who would you rebel against?
Notions of who's really in control

I guess it all depends
But the fact remains
That I AM
The light.
Evident through these illuminated windows of a soul
That was once dark as night,
But those demons took flight.
Couldn't share the space of the spiritual fruits
I started to invite,
The rhetoric of life I recite,
Nor the actual execution of those words
That I highlight.
So, when you see me with
My head held high,
Don't mistake it for
Arrogance or pride
'Cause everyday I am humbled to know,
That for me,
Somebody died.
I just walk like this 'cause.
Well—
When God is your guide
Royalty
Is implied.

Lunar Honey

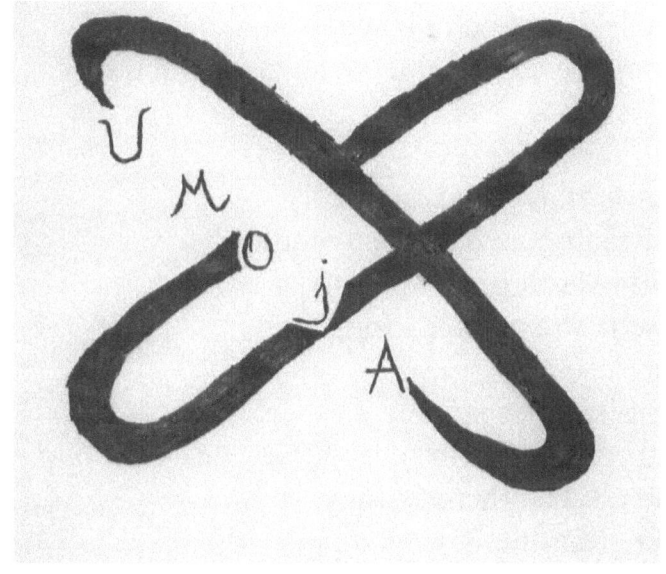

Umoja

How pleasant it is for brothers,
To dwell together in unity.
Pinnacles we need to reach
Can only be achieved if we have this union
And we
Need to seek the needs
Of our brothers who fell weak
In this marginalized race to equity
Handling each life preciously.
'Cause if one of us is losing,
We all lose,
We can't win separately,
And there's no room for indifference,
So, help each other zestfully.
Not, best for me.
Best for we.
Kingdom mindset things
You see,
Our time is near.
Question is,
Are we ALL
Here?

Where You Belong

I've built a chair for you—
And left pieces of the tables,
So that you are able
To continue to build
Your own.
But don't idolize this throne,
Stay focused.
Be mindful of where
The hope is,
Because the hopeless
Will save their best tricks
To derail you
From where you belong.

Holly R. Toomer

ECLIPSE

Lunar Honey

The Solution

Thus formed the solution—
Stop dilutin'.

Holly R. Toomer

Pep Talk

I know you may not know me,
And may be weary of my intentions,
But I see potential in you,
And I think you may have missed it.
I fix crowns, heart muscles,
And specialize in abolition,
I've tripped over your peace,
But I've found the hope to put this in.
For greatness you are destined,
And it's easy to lose sight of this.
Depression,
And systems we're left in,
Make it hard,
To make the light of things.
When the mind gets cloudy,
Nearly impossible to see brighter things,
But sometimes we have to be the photons,
To emit from these wider rings.

So, separate yourself from,
Negativity and misguided beings,
To allow positive influences to guide you,
Through these higher winds.
And don't let anybody make you think,

Lunar Honey

That your life is low,
Like you're not the sons and daughters,
Of the Most High Gawd.

Don't Let Them

Don't let them taint you
Don't let them fake you
And though those demons sound convincing
They don't make you.

Insanity

Repetition is the mother of skill,
But I don't need to repeat pain.
I don't need to repeat the lies I told myself
To make me feel the same.
I elect to be sane.

Soul Food

If you don't have taste for soul food
I'm probably not for you.
Not the edible stuff you eat
But I will shift your mood.
And rewire the mindset
That made you think you could lose.
But my food?
You must
Take your time to chew.
When I say this is for your subconscious
I do not mean to confuse,
But I do mean to renew.

Lunar Honey

Headspace

Already gotta deal with these demons in my head
Telling me that I can't do it,
But then they're in my face too.
It's like a jungle sometimes,
But these trees move.
So I
Cry sweat and bleed proof
Of these deep roots
That run like rivers.
Expected to have a shoulder so cold
But won't quiver
And although I'm not my ancestors
I possess the good spirit
That won't shake.
Identifying false idols
With every correct move I make
Journey too smooth
Sometimes it feels fake
Then I remember whose hands
Lie my fate.

The Trap

Let me start by saying you ARE enough!
It doesn't matter how many pieces
You've broken in to
You can always be picked up
And whether or not your flaws look like mine
Doesn't deny the fact
That you are no less than beautifully designed,
By hands so divine
The heart is inclined
To fuel purpose
And I know we may not be perfect
But no one can be you
Better than you
So being yourself
Is worth it.
You see
I've figured out that
Comparison—is a trap.
That snaps and grabs the beholder looking back,
Or to the side
Or ANYWHERE but STRAIGHT AHEAD
And DOWN THE AISLE.
You see the idea is,
To stay in your lane

Lunar Honey

And I know that sounds like
A narrow-minded thing.
Society has made it sound condescending,
Somewhat limiting.
When in fact
It empowers you to live your dreams.
Keyword: Your
Because it's the soul inside your body
That YOU'RE living for
And the power of life
Lies in the tongue.
So, SAY that you'll win,
And you've won.

Poetry Babe

Poetry, Honey
I don't know a sweeter use of the Word
That flows in me.
I prose in deep
And peruse the pages
Of the baddest to place pen to paper.
My pen's a savior
And she may be your light too,
If you like to listen.
I favor transmuting addictions
To godly glows.
Make your demons your amigos
Cause truth be told,
I aint' ever seen God afraid of His foes
And to conquer you must first
Get
To
Know.
I'm a life-long learner of this.
Grassroot activities
Jump in jump out
Become a turner of this.
There's always work to do—
Poetry.

Lunar Honey

I love you.

DEAR READER AFFIRMING THOUGHTS

#1

I am light and love and this is what I attract.

Lunar Honey

#2

I acknowledge that nothing can hold me back without my permission.

#3

I embrace my desire to impress myself and release my need to impress others.

Lunar Honey

#4

The universe knows and is on my side.

#5

My emotions hold valuable information, so I must get curious about them.

Lunar Honey

#6

It's okay to start over, just start.

#7

I honor God and myself by doing what I love.

Lunar Honey

ABOUT THE AUTHOR

Holly R. Toomer is a poet, educator, certified life coach and artiste from the suburbs of New York. Aside from poetry, she has a passion for music and dance, which she believes, can be healing. Her mission is to illuminate the human condition. As a catalyst for positive change, she believes in having fun while living out one's purpose and she aims to help others to do the same in their lives.

Find out more about Holly Toomer at www.linktr.ee/bellewoodz.

Lunar Honey

This is your reminder that you are amazing.

Holly R. Toomer

Lunar Honey

www.ingramcontent.com/pod-product-compliance
Lightning Source LLC
Chambersburg PA
CBHW020914080526
44589CB00011B/591